"Teaching them to observe all things whatsoever I have commanded you: and, lo, I am with you always, even unto the end of the world". Amen". (St. Matthew 28:20)

J.R. Rogers, Sr. Ministries, Inc.

I0440068

Christian Discipleship, Christian Education

Church Leadership, Seasonal Sermon Series

General Sermon Series, Motivational Studies

Family Studies, Spanish-French-German Books

Dr. Joseph R. Rogers, Sr.

"Teaching them to observe all things whatsoever I have commanded you: and, lo, I am with you always, even unto the end of the world". Amen". (St. Matthew 28:20)

I. Introduction

Joseph R. Rogers, Sr. Ministries, Incorporated is a Christian based ministry designed to share biblical knowledge and insights with the body of Christ in a relevant and informative way. The aim of the ministries is to *develop, equip, mature and advance the body of Christ for kingdom building.*

The bible teaches each us to **acquire knowledge,** through study, **first,** so that we might know The God of The Bible, and **second,** so that learn His principles and precepts.

The bible also teaches us that if we fail to study the Word of God, we become susceptible to the cunning devices and tactics of the Devil.

We are instructed by the greatest Apostle, **Paul of Tarsus,** to arm ourselves with the proper **Christian armor** (Ephesians chapter six). In doing so, we will put on the needed spiritual armor that is required the stand against the wiles and cunning devices of the Devil.

The Devil desire is to sift us as wheat, that is, to **steal, kill** and **destroy.** When we study and apply the Word of God, we are in a nutshell gaining life and that is life more abundant.

If we *study, ingest, digest, properly process and apply God's Word within its* proper **content,** we will then position ourselves to become more than conquerors. If accomplish this, we will lives **VICTORS** and not **VICTIMS.**

2

"Teaching them to observe all things whatsoever I have commanded you: and, lo, I am with you always, even unto the end of the world". Amen". (St. Matthew 28:20)

I have spent over thirty-five (35) years, **studying, referencing, collecting** and **formatting** Christian material with the aim of putting it in simple and understanding form. For What?

That the body of Christ might fulfill the writings of the **Apostle Paul** as he spoke to the Church at Ephesus in chapter four verses 12 -13:

"[12] For the perfecting of the saints, for the work of the ministry, for the edifying of the body of Christ: [13] Till we all come in the unity of the faith, and of the knowledge of the Son of God, unto a perfect man, unto the measure of the stature of the fullness of Christ".

In closing, it is my hope and desire that the material contain in this booklet will **help, develop** and **mature** you, as you move toward your God given **destiny.**

Blessings & Peace,
Joseph R. Rogers, Sr., D. Min.

"Teaching them to observe all things whatsoever I have commanded you: and, lo, I am with you always, even unto the end of the world". Amen". (St. Matthew 28:20)

Table of Contents

"Teaching them to observe all things whatsoever I have commanded you: and, lo, I am with you always, even unto the end of the world". Amen". (St. Matthew 28:20)

"Teaching them to observe all things whatsoever I have commanded you: and, lo, I am with you always, even unto the end of the world". Amen". (St. Matthew 28:20)

"Teaching them to observe all things whatsoever I have commanded you: and, lo, I am with you always, even unto the end of the world". Amen". (St. Matthew 28:20)

II. The Author's Works

A. Church Leadership

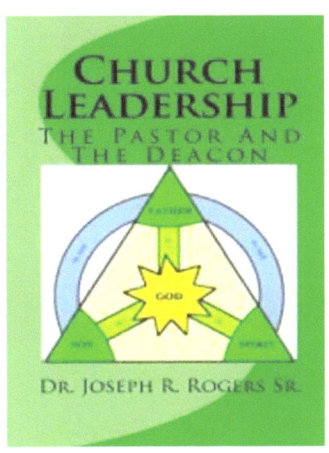

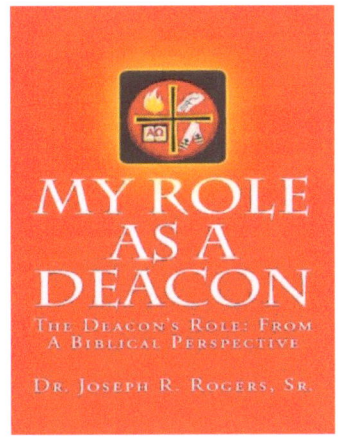

"Teaching them to observe all things whatsoever I have commanded you: and, lo, I am with you always, even unto the end of the world". Amen". (St. Matthew 28:20)

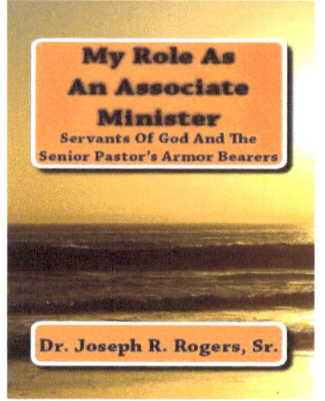

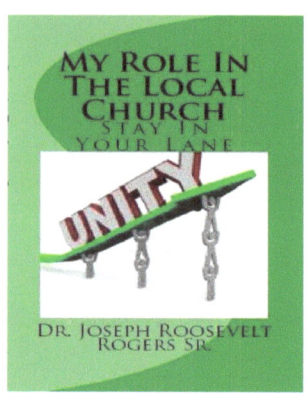

The Above Books Have **'Study Series'**, Except **"My Role In The Local Church"**.

"Teaching them to observe all things whatsoever I have commanded you: and, lo, I am with you always, even unto the end of the world". Amen". (St. Matthew 28:20)

B. Christian Education

"Teaching them to observe all things whatsoever I have commanded you: and, lo, I am with you always, even unto the end of the world". Amen". (St. Matthew 28:20)

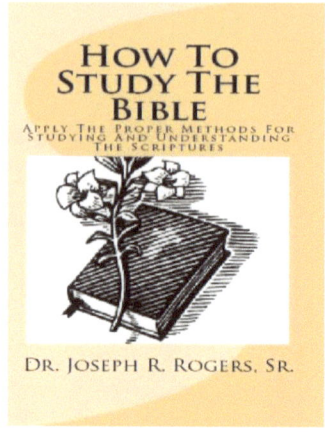

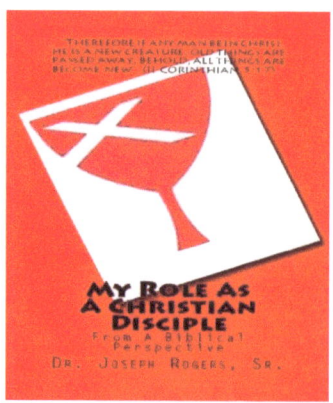

"Teaching them to observe all things whatsoever I have commanded you: and, lo, I am with you always, even unto the end of the world". Amen". (St. Matthew 28:20)

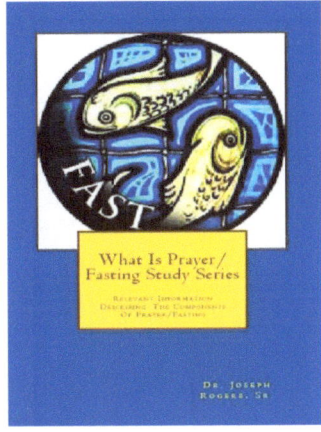

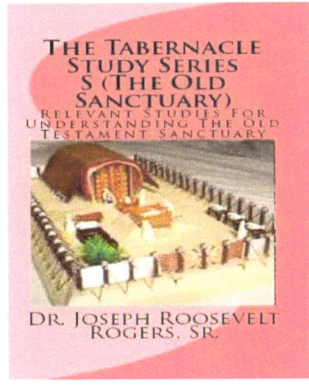

"Teaching them to observe all things whatsoever I have commanded you: and, lo, I am with you always, even unto the end of the world". Amen". (St. Matthew 28:20)

C. General Sermon Series

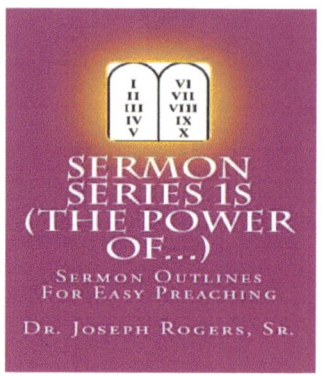

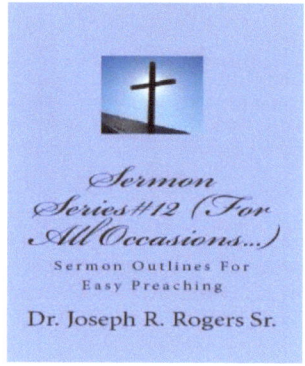

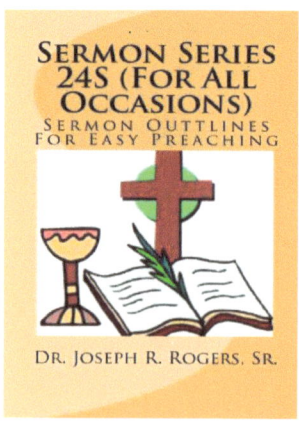

"Teaching them to observe all things whatsoever I have commanded you: and, lo, I am with you always, even unto the end of the world". Amen". (St. Matthew 28:20)

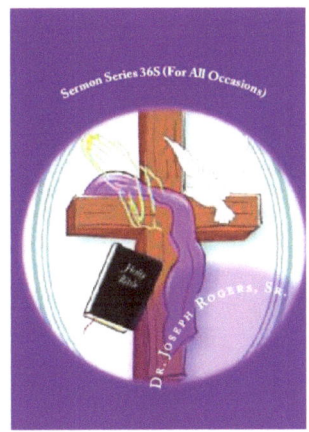
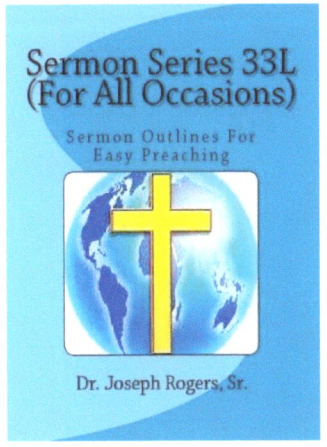

"Teaching them to observe all things whatsoever I have commanded you: and, lo, I am with you always, even unto the end of the world". Amen". (St. Matthew 28:20)

SERMON SERIES
39S (FOR ALL
OCCASIONS)

SERMON OUTLINES FOR
EASY PREACHING

DR. JOSEPH
ROOSEVELT
ROGERS, SR.

"Teaching them to observe all things whatsoever I have commanded you: and, lo, I am with you always, even unto the end of the world". Amen". (St. Matthew 28:20)

D. Seasonal Sermon Outlines

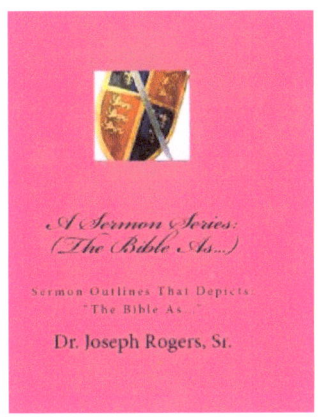

"Teaching them to observe all things whatsoever I have commanded you: and, lo, I am with you always, even unto the end of the world". Amen". (St. Matthew 28:20)

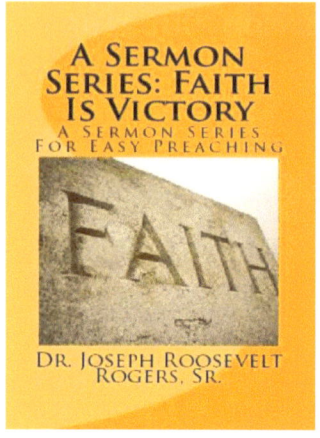

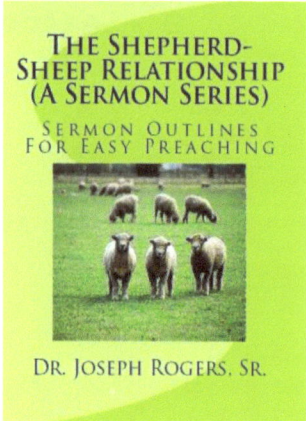

"Teaching them to observe all things whatsoever I have commanded you: and, lo, I am with you always, even unto the end of the world". Amen". (St. Matthew 28:20)

"Teaching them to observe all things whatsoever I have commanded you: and, lo, I am with you always, even unto the end of the world". Amen". (St. Matthew 28:20)

E. Family Series

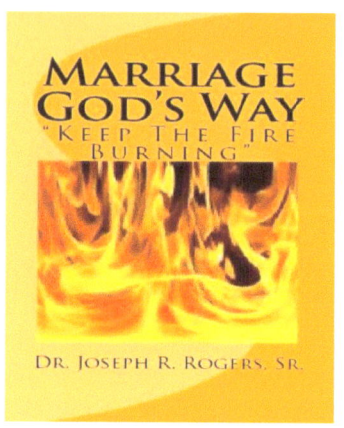

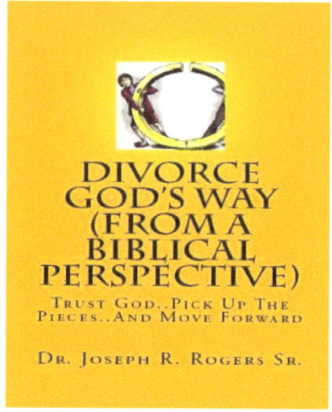

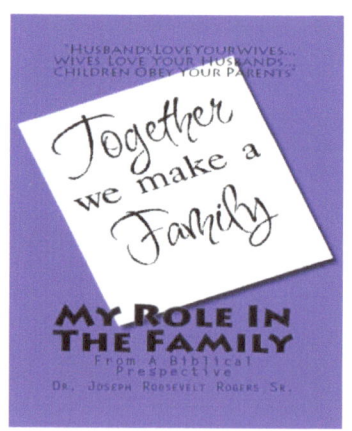

"Teaching them to observe all things whatsoever I have commanded you: and, lo, I am with you always, even unto the end of the world". Amen". (St. Matthew 28:20)

"Teaching them to observe all things whatsoever I have commanded you: and, lo, I am with you always, even unto the end of the world". Amen". (St. Matthew 28:20)

F. Motivational Series:

"Teaching them to observe all things whatsoever I have commanded you: and, lo, I am with you always, even unto the end of the world". Amen". (St. Matthew 28:20)

Motivational Studies Series Con't.

"Teaching them to observe all things whatsoever I have commanded you: and, lo, I am with you always, even unto the end of the world". Amen". (St. Matthew 28:20)

G. Church Guideline/Discipline Series

"Teaching them to observe all things whatsoever I have commanded you: and, lo, I am with you always, even unto the end of the world". Amen". (St. Matthew 28:20)

H. The Senior Ministry Series

"Teaching them to observe all things whatsoever I have commanded you: and, lo, I am with you always, even unto the end of the world". Amen". (St. Matthew 28:20)

J. Memoirs/History Series

24

"Teaching them to observe all things whatsoever I have commanded you: and, lo, I am with you always, even unto the end of the world". Amen". (St. Matthew 28:20)

K. Spanish-German-French Series

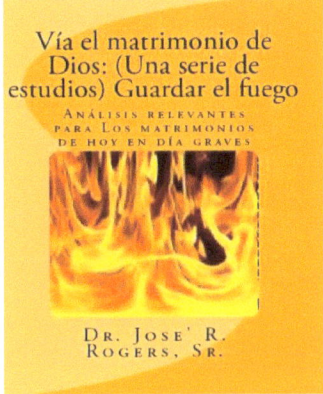

"Teaching them to observe all things whatsoever I have commanded you: and, lo, I am with you always, even unto the end of the world". Amen". (St. Matthew 28:20)

Spanish-German-French Series Con't.

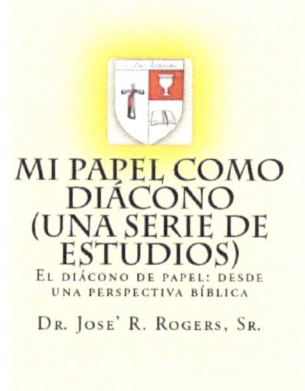

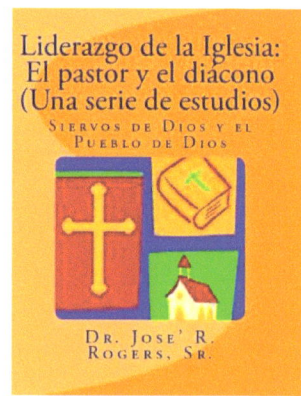

"Teaching them to observe all things whatsoever I have commanded you: and, lo, I am with you always, even unto the end of the world". Amen". (St. Matthew 28:20)

Spanish-German-French Series Con't.

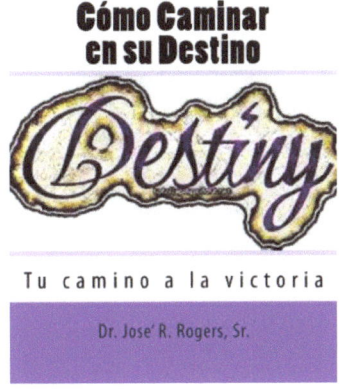

"Teaching them to observe all things whatsoever I have commanded you: and, lo, I am with you always, even unto the end of the world". Amen". (St. Matthew 28:20)

"Teaching them to observe all things whatsoever I have commanded you: and, lo, I am with you always, even unto the end of the world". Amen". (St. Matthew 28:20)

III. A Brief Description Of The Books

A. Church Leadership:

1. Church Leadership: (The Pastor & The Deacon) is a book that defines and describes the role of the only two (2) New Testament church officers. These Leaders are designed look out for the welfare of the local church family.

The pastor is the overall leader and the deacons are selected from the congregation and set aside to assist the pastor with the day to day responsibilities.

The Deacons are not pastors and should not try to be. As the Pastor, the deacons are servants (waiters, assistants). The deacon does not dictate to the pastor nor to the church.

2. The Role Of The Deacon is a book that defines and details the role of the deacon ministry. The Deacons are to following the vote of the local congregation; by carrying out what the majority agrees to do. Deacons are **appointed** and can be **disappointed**. The Deaconship is not transferable from one church to another.

3. The Role Of The Deaconess is a book that defines and describe the role of the local church deaconess from two (2) perspectives:

    a. Tradition Perspective,
    b. Biblical Perspective,

"Teaching them to observe all things whatsoever I have commanded you: and, lo, I am with you always, even unto the end of the world". Amen". (St. Matthew 28:20)

There are a few questions surrounding this role in the local church but the bible is clear and precise as to who deaconess are and their specified duties of the office.

4. The Role Of The Local Church Trustee Ministry a book that defines and describes the role of the church trustee. The Trustees are to always operate within the wishes (vote) of the local church and pastor.

The Trustees are to never take any matter of the church into their own hands. The Trustees are not lords of the finances and real property of the church.

The Trustees' Ministry came into being because of legal matters that have to be dealt with, i.e., contractual responsibilities. The Trustee Ministry is to make sure that church facility is ready for business and worship.

5. The Role Of The Associate Minister is a book that defines and describes the role of the Associate Minister is the local congregation.

The Associate Minister should at no time try to usurp the authority of the senior pastor. The Associate Minster has no power or authority within the local church and should function accordingly.

The Associate Minister should assist the senior pastor as they are ask and never put pressure on the pastor to pray, read the scripture or preach; doing such is disrespectful.

"Teaching them to observe all things whatsoever I have commanded you: and, lo, I am with you always, even unto the end of the world". Amen". (St. Matthew 28:20)

6. The Role Of The Pastor Wife is a book that defines and describes the role of the pastor's wife. The pastor's wife is a very instrumental figure in the local church. The Pastor's Wife must never show favoritism with the congregation; this will only cause division within the family.

Even though this is not an official church office, the pastor wife should be respected by all of the members of the local church family.

The pastor's wife should help in assisting the pastor and church in carrying out its functions, but must she must never try to dictate any of her personal wishes on the church. The Pastor's Wife must at no time come between the pastor and the church's worship or business.

7. My Role In The Local Church is a book that defines and describes the role of each disciple and officer in the local church family. Each church disciple must stay in their proper lanes if the church is be effective and productive.

The church disciples are to always work in harmony; that is, each church member or officer is to remain in their perspective calling or assignments.

When this happens, the church will move along with the least amount of friction and problems. The church is the place of peace, joy, happiness and unity—work to that end!

"Teaching them to observe all things whatsoever I have commanded you: and, lo, I am with you always, even unto the end of the world". Amen". (St. Matthew 28:20)

B. Christian Education

1. Christian Discipleship And The Holy Spirit is a book that defines and describes the role of the Christian as the Power of The Holy Spirit ministers within the body of Christ.

The Holy Spirit fills the believer with power and authority to carry out the mandated of Jesus Christ and mission of the church. The Holy Spirit is 'the promise' the sent from God The Father at the wishes of the Son, Jesus Christ.

Many churches speak little about the third person in the Godhead bodily, but the Holy Spirit is very vital in executing the mission of the New Testament Church.

Without The Holy Spirit (Ghost) we would have no power & authority, no comforter and no guide. He is the in-filler and leader operating in the local church—receive and follow Him!

2. Evangelism 101 is a book that defines and describes the role of Evangelism in the local church setting. Evangelism along with Mission is vital for witnessing to the unbelievers (spiritually) and supplying alms to the needy (physically).

"Teaching them to observe all things whatsoever I have commanded you: and, lo, I am with you always, even unto the end of the world". Amen". (St. Matthew 28:20)

Evangelism is the core of the believer's witness to the world. As a matter of fact, the believer is commanded to go tell the unbelieving world about goodness of Jesus Christ.

3. New Christian Basic Study, My Roles As A New Christian Series, My Role As A Disciple, The Model For A Novice Christian Walk (7, 8, 9, 12) are books that defines and describes what has take place in the heart, mind and soul of each person who has accepted Jesus Christ as Lord and Savior. These books list some very important insights that every believer should know if they are expecting to function successful in the world.

4. The Baptism of The Bible is a book that defines and describes what is **'baptizing'** and the **'different baptisms'** that affects the life of each believer. We also address the question that is asked by some people, that is, **"must a believer be water baptized to be saved".**

There are also references made in the Old & New Testament that describes **'Baptisms'**, namely, John, Moses, Fire, The Cross, and The Believer's.

5. How To Study The Bible is a book that defines and describes the importance of properly studying the bible, that is, line upon line and precept upon precept, always maintaining or keeping all knowledge within its proper contexts.

6. The Book Of Revelation is a book that defines and describes the vision that The Apostle John was privileged to view while exiled on the Isle of Patmos.

"Teaching them to observe all things whatsoever I have commanded you: and, lo, I am with you always, even unto the end of the world". Amen". (St. Matthew 28:20)

The Apostle John was given a vision by God in three parts: **The things which thou hath seen, The things which are and Things which shall be hereafter.**

The Apostle John is shown seven conditions that describe the condition of mankind before the coming of the Lord, Jesus Christ.

This book should be **read, ingested** and **digested** and **apply** by each believer. The unbelievers should receive it as a serious warning. As a matter of fact, **blessed** are those that read and they that hear the words of this prophecy.

11. The Night of Miracles (Christ Birth) is a book that defines and describes the events surrounding the birth of the Lord Jesus Christ.

13. The Tabernacle Study Series is a book that defines and describes the role of the Tabernacle ('Tent') in the wilderness and its relationship to the New Testament Church.

The items in the Tabernacle, has a unique relationship with the New Testament Church and its worship. Some of them are described in this book.

Namely; The High Priest, The Curtain, The Veil, The Lampstands, The Brazen Altar, The Gate, The Laver, The Showbread, The Golden Incense, Holy

> "Teaching them to observe all things whatsoever I have commanded you: and, lo, I am with you always, even unto the end of the world". Amen". (St. Matthew 28:20)

of Holies, Aaron's Rod, and the Ark of the Covenant.

"Teaching them to observe all things whatsoever I have commanded you: and, lo, I am with you always, even unto the end of the world". Amen". (St. Matthew 28:20)

C. General Sermon Series

1. <u>Sermon Series (1-39)</u> are sermon outlines, which covers a variety of topics and subjects. The messages are relevant, theological and biblical sound. All you have to do is add your flavor.

D. <u>Special Sermon Series</u>

1. **The Bible As Sermon Outlines** is a book that describes the different ways and functions that we can apply the Word of God to our lives. The functions describes are: The bible as **A Seed, A Shield, A Sword, A Nail and as A Food.**

2. <u>Men/Fathers Day Sermon Outlines</u> is a book shares insight as to the role of Men/Fathers, as they execute their roles in the family, church and community.

3. <u>Funeral Sermon Outlines</u> is a book that has messages that relates to family bereavement. They are very uplifting and insightful.

4. <u>Worship Sermon Outlines</u> is a book that has messages that relates to how to worship, why we worship and to whom we worship.

5. <u>The Shepherd/Sheep Sermon Outlines</u> is a book that shares the insights to the relationship

"Teaching them to observe all things whatsoever I have commanded you: and, lo, I am with you always, even unto the end of the world". Amen". (St. Matthew 28:20)

of the Shepherd (God) to the Sheep (believer). Psalm 23 is used as a foundation text.

6. <u>Faith Is Victory Sermon Outlines</u> is a book that shares the insights one should have when it comes to dealing with and overcoming the obstacles of life. In this process the absence of faith is a sure defeat.

7. <u>Love Sermon Outlines</u> is a book that describes the different kinds of love and their applications to mankind. Briefly, we have **Eros** (romatic love), **Philo** (friendship love) and **Agape** (God's love).

8. <u>Temptation Sermon Outlines</u> is a book that describes the power of trusting God in times of danger and difficulty. These outlines ensures the believer that whatever he encounter, standing firm on the Word of God will guarantee victory. The Epistle of James is used as a foundation text.

9. <u>Mother's/Women's Sermon Outlines</u> is book that describes the role of women/mothers in the family, church and community. We also talk about their importance.

10. <u>Pastor's Anniversary/Appreciation</u> is a book that describes the role of the pastor and how he/she should be respected, loved and appreciated by the congregation.

"Teaching them to observe all things whatsoever I have commanded you: and, lo, I am with you always, even unto the end of the world". Amen". (St. Matthew 28:20)

E. Family Studies

1. <u>Marriage God's Way</u> is a book that describes the role of the husband and the wife in their relationship in the marriage covenant. It is not a fifty-fifty commitment, but a one-hundred-one hundred per cent effort for both parties.

2. <u>Divorce God's Way</u> is a book that describes how to handle separating once inappropriate things happens after confirming the marriage vows. Some important questions have been asked down through the years when it comes to divorce.

Questions such as: Is it within the will of God to get divorced? Am I bound for life in the relationship? On what grounds is the marriage over? If I separate can I marry some else.

Well, these answers are clear in the bible and this book shares these insights with you.

3. <u>My Role In The Family Pamphlet</u> share short insights as to the role of each family member and how applying them. We can be ensured of a happy, productive and successful relationship if things are done the bible way.

The Roles that are describes in this book are: The Role of The Man/Father; The Role of The wife/Mother; and The Role of The Children.

"Teaching them to observe all things whatsoever I have commanded you: and, lo, I am with you always, even unto the end of the world". Amen". (St. Matthew 28:20)

4. <u>Overcoming The Loss of A Soul Mate</u> is a book that describes in detail some of the events that will be encountered when a wife or husband deceases.

This is a very trying experience and you must approach it from a realistic perspective, if they are expecting to overcome the loss.

Never feel that God is picking on you when this happens. It is easy to fall into that position.

Having experienced this, personally, I believe this book has clear and helpful insight as to what you must do to overcome this challenge.

"Teaching them to observe all things whatsoever I have commanded you: and, lo, I am with you always, even unto the end of the world". Amen". (St. Matthew 28:20)

F. Motivational Studies

1. How To Walk In Your Destiny is a book that is designed to give insights as to how to walk in your God appointed destiny.

God has designed a special pathway for each of us and what we must do is seek His plan for life and walk accordingly.

Even though we have been give the freedom of choice or to choose, there is the perfect plan that God has put into place from the foundation of the world.

2. More Than An Overcomer is my personal auto-biography. It shares with each reader some of my challenging times as well as my times of victory.

Most of all, I want to share with you that it does not matter how you began life but how you processed the challenges and walked in God's will. Be encouraged to know that every obstacle, setback and challenge can be bought under subject with the help of the Lord.

- I was not suppose be born!
- I overcame a terminal illness!
- I overcame an introverted live!
- I overcame the inability to speak publically!
- I became a pastor, educator, writer!

"Teaching them to observe all things whatsoever I have commanded you: and, lo, I am with you always, even unto the end of the world". Amen". (St. Matthew 28:20)

As God did all of this for me, so can He do it for you. Yes! You can become more than an Overcomer!

3. Renewing Your Mind: A Spiritual Inventory is a book that encourages each reader to think positive and with the mind of Christ. This book shares the power of the mind or thinking and the important role it plays in each of our lives.

In order to think properly, we must ingest the word of God on a daily basis. It is the word of God that gives us the proteins and vitamins we need for proper development and maturity.

The bible tells us that as a man thinketh in his heart, so is he. We are challenged by the Apostle Paul as to how we are to think when his address a letter to the Church at Philippi:

He says, *"Finally, brethren, whatsoever things are true, whatsoever things are honest, whatsoever things are just, whatsoever things are pure, whatsoever things are lovely, whatsoever things are of good report; if there be any virtue, and if there be any praise, think on these things".* (Philippians 4:8)

4. Blessed And Highly Favored: (Physically & Spiritually) is a book designed to share insights that are relevant to understanding that God is concerned about the development of the total man: spirit and physical.

It is nothing wrong with desiring the finer things of life. The Lord assures us that in The Epistle of Third John when He says, *"Beloved, I wish above all things that thou mayest prosper and*

"Teaching them to observe all things whatsoever I have commanded you: and, lo, I am with you always, even unto the end of the world". Amen". (St. Matthew 28:20)

be in health, even as thy soul prospereth." (3 John 1:2)

Just remember, that not any of these things belong to you outright. We bought nothing into this world and when we die, we will carry nothing out. Everything belongs to God, and that includes YOU and YOUR THINGS!

5. **From The Pit To The Palace** is a book describing the journey of the African People from African to American as slaves. After having to deal with such horrible conditions God still favored the African Peoples to rise to the top.

The African Peoples are the only people that came to America as slaves. They built this country with their free labor, but God gave them great returns on their investments.

Even until now (2012), The President of The United States is a Blackman, Barak Obama. It is a fact that if you are favored by God there is nothing that will be able to stop you.

6. **Ten Most Wanted Men** is a book designed to help motive those who find themselves in situations that seems to be holding them hostage to the negative things of life. These ten me or motivators, if applied, will help you rise to victory.

7. **Overcoming The Trials of Life** is a book that motives also, but it list five keys that are need to win in your battle with yourself as well as Satan. Sometime we think we know how to handle the situation, but there a mindset that we must possess to overthrow the powers of darkness.

"Teaching them to observe all things whatsoever I have commanded you: and, lo, I am with you always, even unto the end of the world". Amen". (St. Matthew 28:20)

G. Church Discipline Studies

1. **Church Discipline Guidelines** is a book that shares with each reader some important insights as how to handle challenging times in your church family.

We must not allow the devil to take over by being too timid; yet we must not overreact and do more harm than good. Those who choose to walk disorderly in our ranks have to be chastised or reprimanded or we will lose order.

In our churches we must have guidelines in place to handle the situations that run the risk of disrupting the harmony of the local church setting.

H. The Senior Ministry Studies

1. **Insights For The Senior Ministry** is a book that gives very important gems about the aging process. We not only look at aging from a physically perspective, but also from a spiritual perspective.

J. Memoirs Studies

1. **The Memoirs of The Moderator** (1998 – 2010) is a book that describes and details the tenure of Joseph R. Rogers, Sr. as Moderator of The Johnston District Association, consisting of Churches in both, Johnston and Wake Counties.

"Teaching them to observe all things whatsoever I have commanded you: and, lo, I am with you always, even unto the end of the world". Amen". (St. Matthew 28:20)

2. <u>The Life And Legacy Of Willie Rogers, Sr. and Pearlie Graham Rogers</u> is a book detailing the life and legacy of my father and mother.

How they migrated from South Carolina in the latter forties and started afresh in Middlesex, North Carolina. This book details the highs and the lows of things that were endured within the family settings.

This book further most give a detail account of our Mother as she dealt with being a widow at age forty-three (43) and having to raise twelve (12) children alone in 1957.

K. The Spanish-German-French Studies

1. <u>All Of These Books</u> are translated copies of some of the Church Leadership, Christian Education, Motivational and Family Studies.

"Teaching them to observe all things whatsoever I have commanded you: and, lo, I am with you always, even unto the end of the world". Amen". (St. Matthew 28:20)

IV. The Author's Contact Information

Mailing Address:

1313 Ujamaa Drive, Raleigh, NC 27610

Phone No. (919) 208-0200

Email Address:

jroger3420@aol.com

The Author's Works can be ordered online from:

1. Amazon.com
   (Both Paper & Electronic Copies)

2. Createspace.com
   (Paper Copies Only)

3. kdp.amazon.com/
   (Electronic Copies Only)

"Teaching them to observe all things whatsoever I have commanded you: and, lo, I am with you always, even unto the end of the world". Amen". (St. Matthew 28:20)

V. Notes